Cirque du Canard

Malika Pache

BookLeaf
Publishing

Presentation by *BookLeaf Publishing*

Web: www.bookleafpub.com

E-mail: info@bookleafpub.com

ISBN: 978-93-95950-45-9

First edition 2022

To all the clowns of my circus and the squids of my ocean <3

ACKNOWLEDGEMENT

I want to thank my soul friend, Clare Bear. Her unadulterated support of my endeavors is such a crutch I rely on.

Feel His Love

Times I've brushed with death, yet still survived,
I think at the time why?
I look at my life and think worthless,
Yet I survived so why?

I felt his love looking back,
I think my time on earth is not done
there's more I need to do.
More I need to touch or help.

Though living is difficult
there are pockets of happiness and love.
I must still seek them out
where there are none I must create some.

Cow

Crossing the bridge
You bring me joy
Share in your secrets
Don't be coy

I always remember
You over the moon
Maybe it's it
Your opportune

I thank you for
Your non sentient light
Forever on the bridge
My memory bright

You

3

If I could dream again I would be you,
Taste the things you taste,
Feel the things you feel.

If I could dream again I would be you,
Face your fears,
Strengthen your weakness.

If I could dream again I would be you,
You'd never feel alone,
You'd know your worth.

If I could dream again,
I would dream again.

We are

We are the words of the broken
We are the voice of the silent
We are the movement of the still
We are the hope of the dammed

Me

5

ShǎnshǎnFāguāng 闪闪发光,
feilafi,
banjjakbanjjak 반짝반짝,
elikhazimulayo,
Dan,
pikapikahikaru ぴかぴか光る,
gnistrande,
Glittering,
Shining,
Sparkling,
pétillant,
Mousseux,
Gasoso,
Espumoso,
Espumante,
Frizzanti,
Šumivé,
helmeilevä,
scintillante,
súilíneach,
boillsgeach,
pefriog,
köpüklü,
sprankelende,
sachaa,

makinang,
berkilau,
'ōlinolino,
Me.

Chronic

Once it started, the rain,
It burned my skin,
Poured into my soul,
The beginning of my pain.

The life I'd dreamed,
All my hope, desire and future,
Gone before my eyes,
Washed away it seemed.

I tried to cry out,
Though my tears were drowned,
I wanted something to stick,
In vanity I did shout.

Will there be a break?
Droplet after droplet,
Like needles falling,
This is more than I can take.

Darkness of the clouds roll in.
Alone in the downpour,
I close my eyes and open my hands,
Letting the acid cover my skin.

A new sensation touches my hand;
Skin of another, here in the rain,
A soul bound to the same fate,
Here with me to take a stand.

The rain beats on but I'm no longer afraid,
More hands join tightly.
Reassurance in fear and and strength,
A future to no not evade.

Gaslight

9

How much did you say that I learned my
lessons?
How did much did you say this was all dream?
I know it's wrong,
wrong from the way I'm hurting.
I know it's real from the way I scream.

Abyss

Cold warmth cloaks me
Never ending, forever.
They said it would be lonely,
An indescribable terror.

I love it here.
I will stare into you for hours,
Never once feeling fear.
This moment truly ours.

I wonder of your layers,
I wonder of this blank space.
They will keep me in their prayers;
Yet you keep me in your embrace.

Twisted Marionette

You parade in the masquerade of sin.

Your smirk drawn by the stings of fate.

You can act but cannot act alone.

The lie of agency, you wear it well.

The illusion of free will wills your movements.

Your double, believable en masse but is weak between the cracks.

Your grand design is funny; considering the author.

Maybe you have layers, and yet couldn't choose their arrangement.

Best friend

Friend I know you're hurting,
You say you want to die;
And I know it won't help,
If I say so do I.

May I be selfish
Even if only for a time;
When I say I want you with me,
You're the greatest friend of mine?

Cake

I want to eat the cake,
It's looks fluffy and firm.

I want to eat the cake,
It has 2 layers all for me.

I want to eat the cake,
When I see it dressed so prettily.

I want to eat the cake,
Till I am sick of the sweetness.

I want to eat the cake,
And squish with both hands.

I want to eat the cake,
You're hiding in your pants.

Remember Where is Home

It's not in the destination no matter how far
roam.
You'll find it in good vibrations,
And moments that touch your soul.

You'll find it in the people and their smiles that
they shine
They'll offer you place in heart where you can
spend your time

Home is not static, stuck in only one place
Home is fluid and flexible and it connot be
replaced

The idea of home can be scary if you are going it
alone
But know you have a place in me. A place to
call home.

Thank You

I found you
A great part of me
Another piece of the puzzle
Of my genealogy.

I was nervous
As nervous as could be
Almost paralysed with a fear
A fear that you would reject me.

That was all for nothing
Some may even call it silly
With a warm smile and big hug
You welcomed me.

Clown

Constant fear of rejection, a fear that none will
accept me.
Love has come and gone though I wish you'd
stay with me.
Only fools are left here, with nowhere else to
hide.
Words of wisdom comfort me no matter how
they lied.
No-one knows the true feelings the fills me with
great glee.

Twin 17

From the moment I saw you
I knew I'd adore you
I am always here for you
To always reassure you

I see you struggling
I see you hurting
This for me is disconcerting
I know you're rising
I know shining
This for me is so inspiring

From the moment I saw you
I knew I'd adore you
I am always here for you
To always reassure you

Feelings

I feel like I want to cry

I feel overwhelmed, like I can't breathe

I feel miserable about myself

I feel unloved, undeserving

I feel alone and isolated

I feel the sleepless nights

I feel anxious

I feel like I don't want to socialise

I feel blurry, like I don't exist

I feel like nothing matters

I feel like my heart is sunken

Oneness

Manifesting all I want, all I need.
Making real that which isn't.
Bringing life to the lifeless.
Allowing the existence in this reality.

Connection to all.
Understanding the relationship of us and mother earth.
Relating patterns to join everything.
Joined in peaceful harmony.

Purpose of our time here.
To exist is enough.
Don't waste time questioning meaning.
Waste time having fun.

Grounded and calm.
Safe from all that causes harm.
In touch with my feelings.
Present in the moment.

Healing ourselves
The world is ill with no cure.
It's still possible to manage the symptoms.
We are allowed to rest.

Men

The rogues are following false profits
Worried about identity erosion
Social constructs delivering anxiety
Feelings you bury down

Comfort in your echo Chambers
Suffocating toxic claustrophobia
Worried your position is becoming weaker
But is the opposite truly weak?

The binary infight is harmful
That's what is hurting you
Though there are 2 on each side
They are completely intertwined

Fighting against true nature
Stuck in your rigid land
The view of the crisis is clouded
There is hope in worth

Being awake is not the issue
Though insomnia hurts
The false prophets are not you're friends
You are human and loved

www.ingramcontent.com/pod-product-compliance
Lightning Source LLC
Chambersburg PA
CBHW061329140726
47998CB00007B/2613